HEALTHY BODY

Diet and Your Body

Alison Cooper

WAYLAND

This book is based on the original title *How Does My Diet Affect Me?* by Patsy Westcott, in the *Health and Fitness* series, published in 1999 by Hodder Wayland

This differentiated text edition is written by Alison Cooper and published in Great Britain in 2005 by Hodder Wayland, an imprint of Hodder Children's Books.

This paperback edition published in 2007 by Wayland, an imprint of Hachette Children's Books.

© Copyright 2005 Wayland

Editor: Kirsty Hamilton
Designer: Jane Hawkins
Consultant: Jayne Wright

Picture acknowledegments
Digital Vision 13 bottom, 15 top, 16-17, 19, 23 top, 27, 28 top; The Healthy Alliance/CCH Communications 8; Image Bank 39 (Juan Silva); Science Photo Library 14 (Adrienne Hart-Davis), 17 top left (Gaillard, Jerrican), 18 (Sheila Terry), 20 (Tony Craddock), 21 (Quest), 25 (BSIP Laurent H Americain), 28 bottom, (Damian Lovegrove), 32 (Clinical Radiology Dept, Salisbury District Hospital), 33 (Steve Horrell), 34 (John Bavosi, 43 (John Greim), 44 top (Dr P Marazzi), 44 bottom (Adrienne Hart-Davis), 45 (BSIP Edwige); Tony Stone Images 1 (Timothy Shonnard), 4 Elie Bernager, 5 (Lori Adamski Peek), 6 (Leland Bobbe), 7 (Christopher Bissell), 10 (Ian Shaw), 12 (John Kelly), 13 top (Yann Layma), 17 top right (Christel Rosenfeld), 22-23 (Paul Chesley), 24 (Rosemary Weller), 26 (Warren Rosenberg), 30 (Dennis O'Clair), 31 (Lori Adamski Peek), 35 (Frank Siteman), 36 (Paul Webster), 37 (Ian O'Leary), 38 (Paul Redman), 40 (Steven Peters), 40-41 (Donna Day), 42 (Peter Cade). The illustration on page 15 is by Peter Bull.

All possible care has been taken to trace the ownership of each photograph and to obtain permission for its use. If there are any omissions or if any errors have occurred, they will be corrected in subsequent editions, on notification to the publisher.

British Library Cataloguing in Publication Data
Cooper, Alison, 1967 –
Diet and your body. – Differentiated ed. - (Healthy body)
1. Nutrition - Juvenile literature 2.Diet - Juvenile
literature
I. Title
613.2

ISBN-13: 978 0 7502 5089 4

Printed in China

Wayland,
an imprint of Hachette Children's Books
338 Euston Road, London NW1 3BH

Contents

Why We Need Food

The type and amount of food that you usually eat is called your diet. Eating a good variety of foods will help to keep your body strong and healthy throughout your life. It's also important not to eat too much, or too little.

Your body needs nutrients to make it grow and work properly. You get these nutrients from food. Your body also needs food to give you energy.

You don't just need energy for activities such as running, cycling and swimming. Your body also needs it for vital jobs such as breathing and to keep your heart beating.

The energy in food is measured in units called calories. A slice and a half of bread contains about 100 calories.

Your body uses up more energy when you are doing a physical activity, like roller-blading, than when you are sitting still. ▶

◀ Different people need different amounts and types of food. It depends on whether you are a child or an adult, a boy or a girl, and whether you use a lot of energy in your job.

A Balanced Diet

Your body cannot get all the nutrients it needs from just one type of food. You need to eat a variety of foods, in the right amounts. This is called a balanced diet.

Around the world, people get the nutrients they need from different foods. It depends on the crops they can grow or the animals they keep, or on the type of food they can afford to buy.

Some people avoid certain foods for religious reasons. For example, Muslims do not eat pork, while Hindus do not eat beef. Strict rules govern the foods that Jews can eat and the way it is prepared. These restrictions do not prevent people from having a balanced diet because they can get all the nutrients they need from other foods.

Food and the rituals linked to it are important for Jewish people. ▼

▲ When you exercise, you need to replace the water you lose through sweating.

Water for life

You can survive for several weeks without food, but only a few days without water. Water helps you to digest food and flushes waste products through your body. It is lost when you sweat or pass urine.

You can replace water by drinking several glasses of water every day. Eating fruit and vegetables also helps because they contain water, too.

Types of nutrients

Your body needs quite large amounts of protein, fats and carbohydrates. These nutrients help your body to grow and repair itself, and give you energy. Vitamins and minerals keep the cells of your body working properly. You only need tiny amounts of these but they are vital for your health.

Food groups

Foods are divided into five groups, based on the nutrients they provide:

- bread, other cereals and potatoes
- fruit and vegetables
- milk and dairy foods
- meat, fish and alternatives
- fatty and sugary foods.

Bread, other cereals and potatoes
Food in this group provides carbohydrates, vitamins, minerals and fibre. Aim to eat at least six portions each day.

Fruit and vegetables
These provide carbohydrates, protein, minerals, vitamins and fibre. Try to eat five portions of fruit and vegetables every day.

Meat, fish and alternatives
Meat, fish, eggs, dried beans and peas, lentils and nuts contain protein, vitamins and minerals. Try to eat two portions a day from this group.

Fatty and sugary foods
This group includes sweets, biscuits, crisps, cakes, ice cream and sweet drinks. You should only eat these occasionally, and only in small amounts.

Milk and dairy foods
Yoghurt, cheese and milk provide protein, vitamins and minerals. Aim to eat three portions a day.

▲ There are no 'good' or 'bad' foods but getting the right balance is very important.

Fatty and sugary foods contain a lot of calories but not many nutrients. Your body stores calories it doesn't need as fat and eventually you become overweight. This puts a strain on your body.

Dos and Don'ts for your Diet

DO

• Enjoy your food. • Eat a variety of food.
• Eat enough food to keep you at a healthy weight.
• Eat plenty of foods such as bread, cereal and potatoes.
• Eat plenty of fruits and vegetables.

DON'T

• Eat regularly foods that contain a lot of fat.
• Have sugary foods and drinks too often.

▲ You need more energy and nutrients during your teens.

Food for growth

At around the age of ten, girls begin a growth spurt, when they get taller and put on weight. For boys, the growth spurt begins a little later, when they are about twelve. A good diet is essential at this stage in your life.

Protein foods such as meat, fish and lentils help your muscles to grow. Calcium, from milk, cheese and yoghurt, makes your bones strong. The amount of blood in your body increases as you grow, so you need iron for healthy red blood cells. You can get iron from meat, oily fish and dark green vegetables.

Girls put on fat during their teens and boys lose fat. Girls lose blood each month once their periods start so they need to top-up their iron levels. Girls and boys need slightly different diets because of the different ways their bodies are changing.

- Between eleven and fourteen, you need about 2,220 calories a day if you are a boy. If you are a girl, you need about 1,845 calories a day.

- During the growth spurt, you can expect to grow an average of 23 cm taller. You will gain between 20 and 26 kilograms in weight.

The blue area on these charts shows the normal range of heights and weights for boys and girls at different ages. The green line shows the average height or weight. ▼

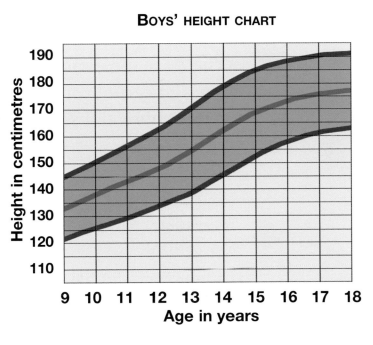

BOYS' HEIGHT CHART

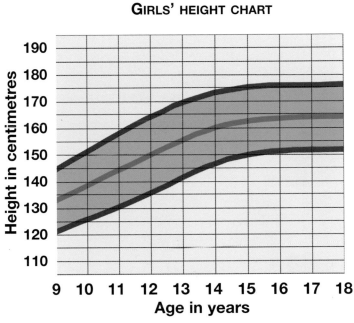

GIRLS' HEIGHT CHART

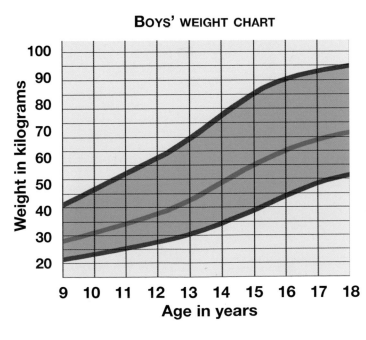

BOYS' WEIGHT CHART

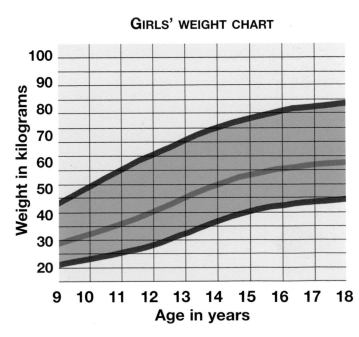

GIRLS' WEIGHT CHART

Energy

▲ All types of bread contain starch.

Carbohydrates

Your body gets most of its energy from foods called carbohydrates. There are three main types of carbohydrate: starch, fibre and sugar.

Starch

Starch is called a complex carbohydrate. Your body breaks it down very slowly, so the energy it contains is released over several hours. It keeps your energy at a steady level. You get starch from foods such as bread, pasta, rice and yams.

Fibre

Fibre is a complex carbohydrate, too. Insoluble fibre is sometimes called roughage. You get it from bran and the skins and seeds of fruit and vegetables. It helps to prevent constipation.

▲ In many parts of the world people get most of their carbohydrates from rice.

There is another type of fibre, called soluble fibre. You get this from most fruit and vegetables, beans, lentils, porridge oats, rye bread and barley. It helps to keep down the level of cholesterol in your blood. This is important because it helps to prevent heart disease. It also helps to keep your energy levels steady. You need to eat foods that provide your body with soluble and insoluble fibre.

13

Types of sugar

Sugar is a simple carbohydrate. Your body breaks it down quickly. There are different types of sugar. One type is glucose, which is found in honey, fruit and vegetables. Your body can release the energy from glucose

▲ If you like sweets, it's best to have them only as an occasional treat.

straightaway. The other types of sugar have to be turned into glucose inside your body before your body can use them.

Sweets and chocolate: bad news for your body

Eating sweets gives you a burst of energy. This is because your body absorbs the sugar in them quickly. The trouble is, you use up the energy quickly and soon feel tired.

Another problem with eating sweets is that the sugar causes tooth decay. Some people have an allergic reaction to the artificial colours and flavours in them. They might get headaches, coughs or rashes.

Chocolate is not as bad for you as sweets. It contains some protein and minerals. There are also chemicals in it that help to make you feel good and alert. The bad news is that chocolate contains a lot of sugar and fat, so if you eat a lot of it, you will put on weight.

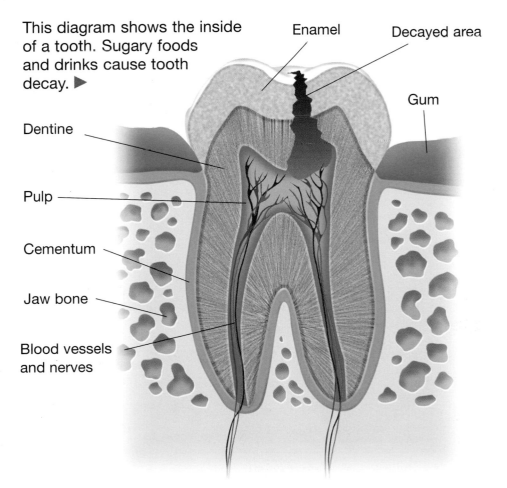

This diagram shows the inside of a tooth. Sugary foods and drinks cause tooth decay. ▶

Enamel

Decayed area

Gum

Dentine

Pulp

Cementum

Jaw bone

Blood vessels and nerves

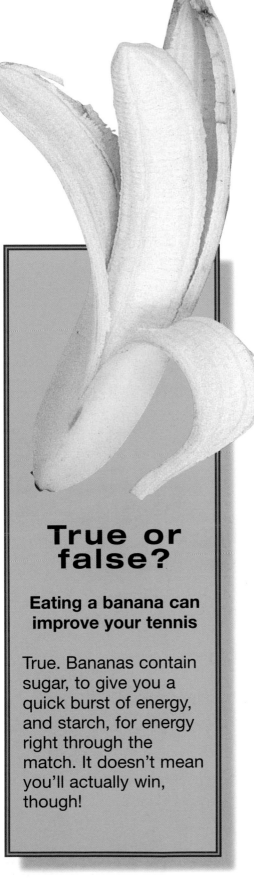

True or false?

Eating a banana can improve your tennis

True. Bananas contain sugar, to give you a quick burst of energy, and starch, for energy right through the match. It doesn't mean you'll actually win, though!

15

Protein

What is protein for?

You need protein to grow and to help your body to repair itself if it becomes damaged. It supports your body by forming part of your bones and muscles. Protein also helps your body to fight off infections.

All fish are a good source of protein and other nutrients. ▼

Amino acids

Before your body can use protein, it has to be broken down into simple substances called amino acids. There are 20 amino acids in protein. Your body can make most of them by itself but there are eight amino acids that you can only get from food.

▲ Shellfish, such as prawns, crabs and lobsters, are rich in amino acids.

Beans and lentils provide some of the amino acids your body cannot make for itself. ▶

Protein for energy

If you don't get enough energy from your food, your body changes amino acids into sugar in your blood. This provides you with more energy. If you eat more protein than your body needs, it can be stored as fat.

Protein from food

Meat, fish, eggs, dairy products and soya products (such as soya milk) contain all eight of the amino acids your body cannot make for itself. Cereals, nuts, lentils and beans contain some of these too.

Getting enough protein

If you are a vegetarian, you can get the eight essential amino acids from soya products. You can also combine foods to get the amino acids you need. Baked beans on toast, for example, give you some protein from the beans and some from the wheat in the bread.

▲ Eggs provide vegetarians with essential amino acids.

Which foods provide protein?

Meat or fish eaters	Vegetarians
Chicken	Baked beans
Turkey	Haricot beans
Rabbit	Soya beans and soya
Ham	products (e.g. tofu, miso,
Beef	soya milk)
Pork	Broad beans
Lamb	Aduki beans
Salmon	Hazelnuts
Trout	Brazil nuts
Cod	Cheese
Tuna	Eggs

Protein for exercise

Some people think that athletes need extra protein. In fact, athletes really need extra carbohydrates to give them energy. Weightlifters and body-builders do need more protein because it helps to build up their muscles. They should be able to get the extra protein they need by eating a balanced diet.

Extra carbohydrates give you extra energy – to make you a winner! ▶

Fat

Fat is packed with energy. It helps to make your food taste better. It also gives it a better flavour and smell. Some types of fat contain nutrients that help you to grow. They also help certain parts of your body to develop, such as your brain. There is a layer of fat under your skin that helps to keep you warm.

Unsaturated fats

Fats and oils from fish, seeds, nuts and vegetables are called unsaturated fats. They provide your body with nutrients called 'essential fatty acids'.

Fish and chips contain a lot of saturated fat, so don't eat them too often. ▶

Fat from fish

Oily fish, such as mackerel, fresh tuna, sardines and salmon, contain fatty acids that help to keep you healthy. However, girls should eat no more than two 140g portions of oily fish per week; boys can eat up to four portions. This is because pollution that builds up in the bodies of these fish can damage people's health.

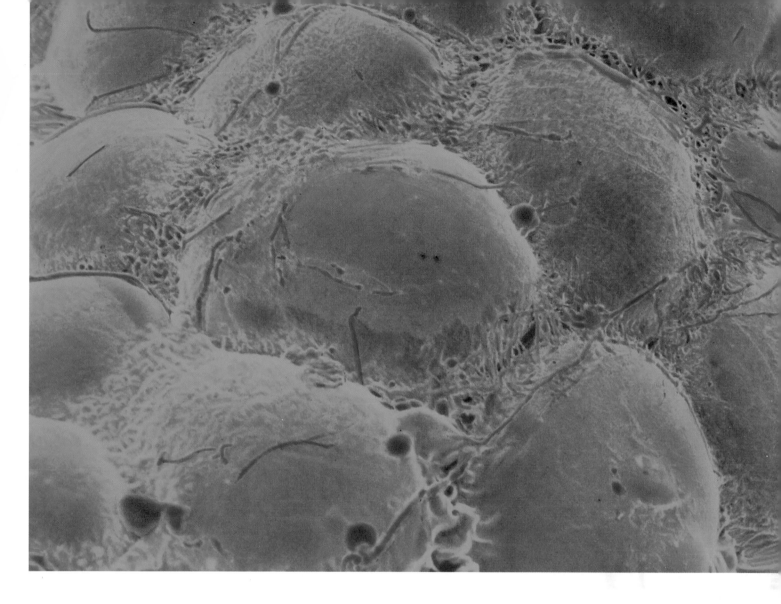

Saturated fats

Saturated fats mainly come from animals. They include butter, lard, cheese and fats in meat, which are usually hard at room temperature. Eating a lot of saturated fats can increase the risk of heart disease when you are older. Fried foods and red meats contain high levels of saturated fats. Choose lean meat, chicken and turkey when you can.

▲ This picture shows the fat cells under your skin. The picture has been magnified 750 times.

Cakes and crisps

Cakes, biscuits, pies and sauces like mayonnaise contain trans fats. These might also increase the risk of heart disease. It is sensible not to eat them too often.

Vitamins and Minerals

Your body only needs tiny amounts of vitamins and minerals but they do a vital job. Fruit and vegetables are rich in vitamins and minerals, so you need to include plenty of them in your diet. They help to make sure that the chemical changes that take place inside your body work properly.

A wide variety of fresh fruit and vegetables are on sale at this market in Malaysia. ▼

Essential jobs

Each vitamin or mineral has its own special job to do. Vitamin C helps you to fight off infections. Iron, which is a mineral, keeps your blood healthy. Vitamins and minerals work together, as well as doing their own jobs. For example, vitamin C helps your body to absorb iron.

Eat your greens!

▲ Make sure you include plenty of leafy green vegetables in your diet.

Green vegetables such as spinach and cabbage contain a lot of vitamin C. Dark-green leafy vegetables also contain a vitamin called folic acid, which your body needs to make new cells.

DID YOU KNOW?

People who smoke need more vitamin C than non-smokers. This is because smoking reduces the amount of vitamin C that is available to do its normal job inside the body.

Getting enough vitamins

Vitamin C and the B group vitamins (see below) dissolve in water. If you cook vegetables by boiling them, most of the vitamins dissolve into the cooking water. Steaming the vegetables keeps in more of the vitamins.

◄ Eating raw fruit and vegetables in a salad is a good way to get vitamin C.

Vital vitamins

VITAMIN	WHY YOU NEED IT	WHERE TO FIND IT
A	Growth	Tuna, herring, mackerel, liver, kidneys, milk, eggs, cheese, margarine, butter
Beta-carotene	May help the body to fight against some types of cancer	Carrots, broccoli, spinach, cabbage, oranges, tomatoes, red and yellow peppers, pumpkins, squash, sweet potatoes, cantaloupe and ogen melons
B group vitamins	Growth and development, healthy nervous system, digestion, converting food into energy	Liver, yeast extract, meat, milk, yoghurt, cheese, butter, eggs, fish, whole-grain cereals, dark-green vegetables, Brazil nuts, pistachio nuts, walnuts, beans, bananas
C	Healthy teeth, bones, skin; helps the body absorb iron	Fruit and vegetables especially citrus fruits, blackcurrants, strawberries, peppers and potatoes
D	Helps the body absorb calcium and phosphorus for healthy bones and teeth	Fish liver oils, eggs, margarines with added vitamins, tuna, salmon, sardines
E	Protects against heart disease	Vegetable oils, nuts, seeds, margarine
K	Needed to make the blood clot properly	Green leafy vegetables, especially cabbage, broccoli, Brussels sprouts

Some vitamins dissolve in fat inside your body. These are vitamins A, D, E, K and beta-carotene. They are stored mainly in your liver.

Vitamin deficiencies

If your body does not get the vitamins it needs, you could develop a disease or other health problems. For example, until about 300 years ago, sailors on long voyages used to get a disease called scurvy. They did not get enough vitamin C because there were no fresh fruit and vegetables on board ship. When doctors discovered what the problem was, ships started to carry limes and lemons so that everyone could get enough vitamin C.

This skin specialist is examining a woman's skin through a magnifying lens. Vitamins are essential for healthy skin. ▼

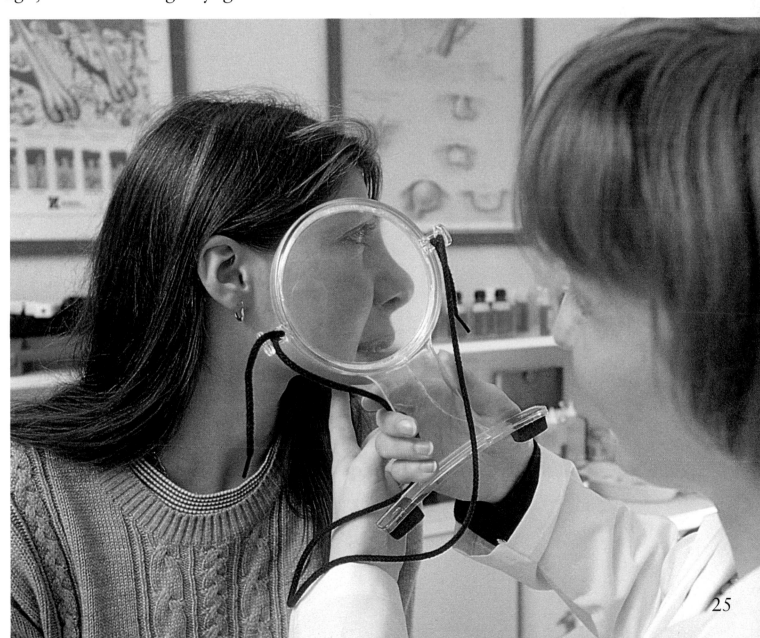

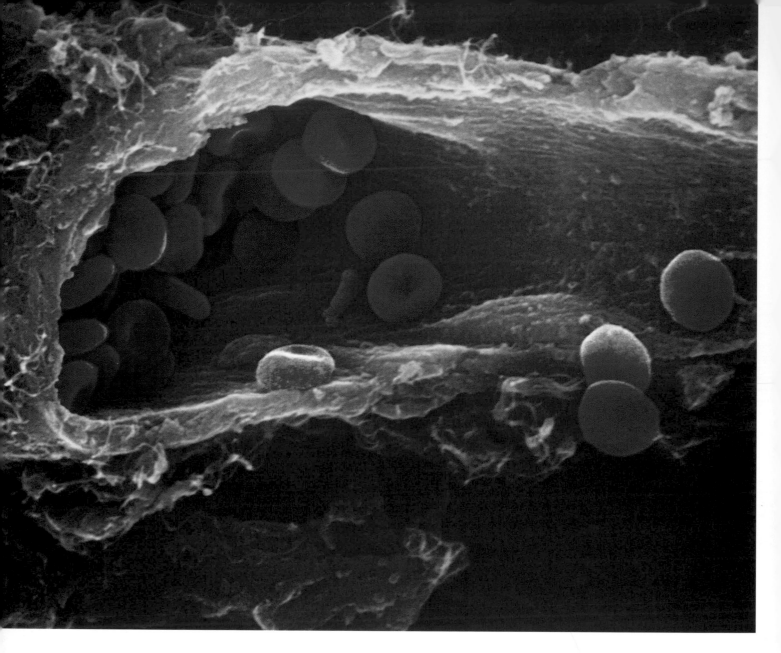

▲ This picture shows red blood cells passing through a vein. It has been magnified many times.

Why do we need minerals?

Your body needs minerals so that it can carry out important processes. Some minerals help to balance the fluid levels in your body. Others become part of your bones, teeth and muscles.

If you don't get enough minerals from your diet, you could become ill. For example, anaemia is a disease of the blood that people develop when they don't get enough iron. It makes you feel weak and tired.

Iron

Iron is especially important during your teenage years. Your body is growing and making more blood. Iron helps to make healthy red blood cells, which carry oxygen to every part of your body.

You can get iron from meat, fish and poultry. You can also get it from dark-green vegetables and dried fruit such as apricots. Iron is added to many breakfast cereals and breads as well.

Vitamin C helps your body to absorb iron, so eating fruit or drinking fruit juice with a meal rich in iron is a good idea. ▼

True or false?

Milk is good for you

True. Milk contains a lot of calcium, so drinking milk is an excellent way of helping your bones to develop. As they get older, people's bones sometimes become brittle and break easily. Eating a diet that is rich in calcium throughout your life helps to prevent this.

Calcium

Calcium is another mineral that is very important during your teens. Almost half your adult skeleton forms during adolescence and your bones are mainly made up of calcium. You can get calcium from milk and dairy foods. You need three servings a day – a glass of milk, a yoghurt or a chunk of cheese.

▲ Shellfish contain iodine, which is needed for healthy growth.

You can also get calcium from bread, beans, nuts, seeds, dried fruit and green leafy vegetables. It is harder for your body to absorb calcium from these foods than from dairy foods. One way to help your body absorb the calcium is to eat foods containing vitamin D at the same time, such as oily fish, margarine, eggs and breakfast cereals.

◄ Drinking milk helps you to have strong, healthy teeth, as well as healthy bones.

Magic minerals

MINERAL	WHY YOU NEED IT	WHERE TO FIND IT
Calcium	Healthy bones and teeth, helps blood to clot	Milk and dairy foods, nuts, sesame seeds, broccoli
Fluorine	Healthy teeth and bones	Seafood, sea salt, tap water
Iodine	Helps to keep the thyroid gland working properly (the thyroid gland is involved in growth and the release of energy in the body)	Seafood, seaweed
Iron	Healthy blood, especially red blood cells	Liver, kidneys, sardines, dark-green vegetables, apricots, breakfast cereals
Magnesium	Healthy bones and teeth, healthy nerves and muscles	Whole-grain cereals, nuts, dried peas and beans, sesame seeds, dried figs, green vegetables
Phosphorus	Healthy bones and teeth, helps to release energy from cells, helps the body absorb other nutrients	Milk, cheese, meat, fish, poultry, nuts, seeds, cereals
Potassium	Helps to keep fluid levels steady in the body, helps to keep the heartbeat regular and control blood pressure	Bananas, avocados, potatoes, seeds, nuts
Zinc	Growth, sexual development, helps the body to fight off infections	Oysters, red meat, peanuts, sunflower seeds

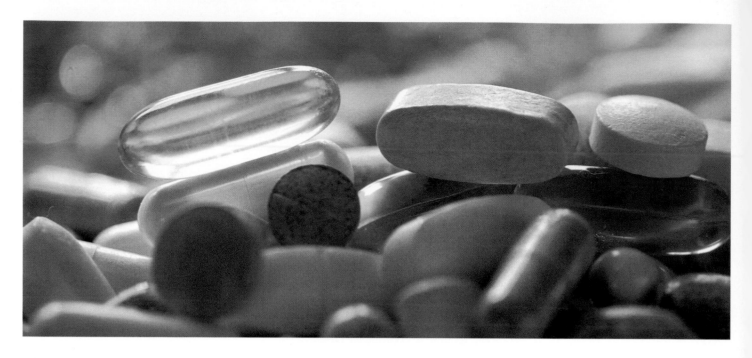

▲ Food supplements can be taken as tablets, capsules or drops.

Food supplements

Sometimes people need to take food supplements because they are not getting enough nutrients from their diet. People who have to avoid certain foods because they need to lose weight might need a supplement containing vitamins and minerals. Vegans are people who do not eat any animal products. They might need to take a vitamin B12 supplement because vitamin B12 is only found naturally in food that comes from animals.

Dangers of supplements

Your body cannot get rid of vitamins that dissolve in fat, such as vitamin A and vitamin D. If there is too much vitamin A in your body it can damage your liver. Too much vitamin D can lead to problems with the heart and kidneys. This is why it is important not to take too many food supplements.

Some sports drinks and foods claim to give you more energy but a healthy diet should give you all the strength and energy you need. ▶

Healthy Eating for Life

Eating too many foods that contain a lot of fats and sugars usually makes you overweight. It can lead to high blood pressure, which is dangerous for your body, and heart disease. The good news is that there are many substances in food that can actually protect you against disease.

This x-ray image shows the hands of a person suffering from rheumatoid arthritis. This is a painful disease of the joints. Some doctors think food allergies may help to cause rheumatoid arthritis. ▼

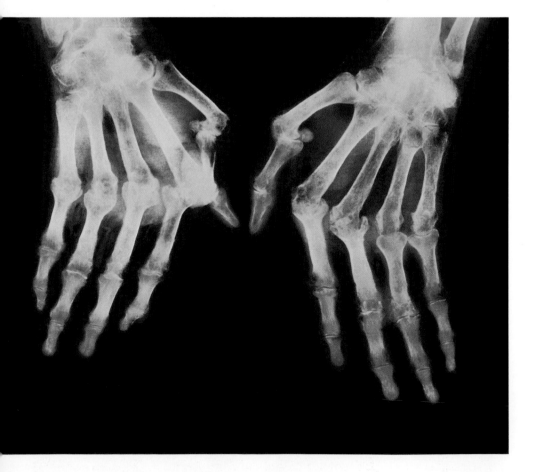

ACE vitamins!

Beta-carotene, Vitamin C and vitamin E are sometimes called the 'ACE' vitamins. The 'A' is for vitamin A because beta-carotene is changed into vitamin A inside your body. The ACE vitamins help to keep your cells healthy by destroying substances called free radicals. Free radicals can damage cells and so lead to disease.

Healthy eating

People living around the Mediterranean have low levels of heart disease and cancer. Their healthy diets include a lot of fruit and vegetables, a little fish and meat, olive oil and a small amount of wine.

▲ This health practitioner is choosing ingredients for a medicine. Traditional Chinese medicine uses plant chemicals to treat disease.

DID YOU KNOW?

People have used plants to treat illness for thousands of years. Now scientists have found chemicals in plants that act like medicines and help the body to fight disease.

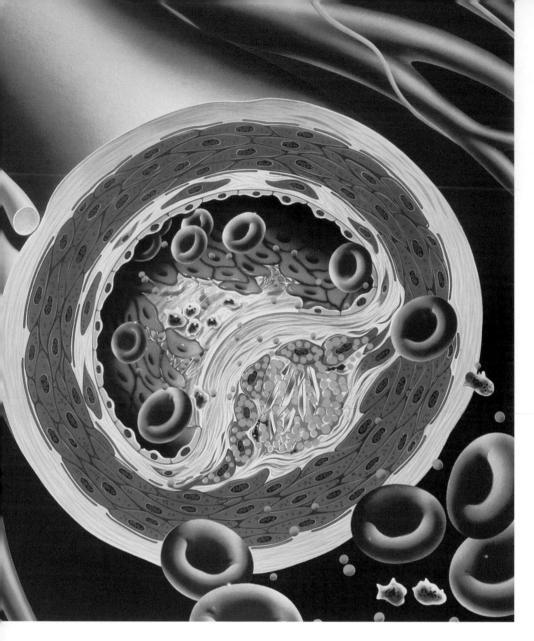

◀ This picture shows the inside of an artery. Cholesterol (coloured yellow in the picture) has built up in the artery. The space that is left for the blood to pass through has become narrower.

Diabetes

Diabetes is a disease that people get when their bodies do not produce enough insulin. Insulin is a chemical that controls the level of sugar in the blood. People with diabetes need a diet that is high in starch and fibre but low in sugar and fat. This helps to make sure their blood sugar does not rise too high or drop too low.

Heart disease

Cholesterol is a fatty substance that sticks to blood vessels called arteries and clogs them up. This is one of the causes of heart attacks. Foods that are high in saturated fats and trans fats raise the level of cholesterol in the blood. This is why it is important not to eat too much butter, fatty meat, pies and cakes.

Protection against cancer

Cancer is a very serious disease. It is caused when some cells in the body divide and grow faster than they should. Some experts think the food you eat can help protect you against cancer. Make sure your diet gives you plenty of ACE vitamins (see page 32) and fibre. Avoid eating a lot of meat, especially red meat.

Organic food

Most farm crops are sprayed with chemicals to kill weeds and insect pests. Farm animals are often given substances to make them grow faster. Some people think it is healthier to eat organic food, which is produced without using such chemicals.

Try not to eat barbecued food that has been charred black. Burning produces harmful substances that could cause cancer. ▼

Vegetarianism

Vegetarians are people who don't eat meat, poultry, game or fish. They don't eat products that are made from animals after they have been killed, such as gelatine or lard. Some vegetarians do eat food that is produced by animals, such as milk and eggs. Vegans don't eat any foods that come from animals at all.

People choose to be vegetarians for many different reasons. A person's religion might forbid eating meat. Some people think it is better for their health, or they don't like the taste of meat and fish. Others believe the way animals are raised to provide food for people is cruel.

A healthy diet without meat

If you are vegetarian, it is important to eat a wide variety of foods – not just fruit and vegetables but also cereals, seeds, nuts, beans, peas and a small amount of fat.

Vegans need to eat foods that have vitamin B12 added to them. This is because the vitamin is only found naturally in food that comes from animals. You might also need to take calcium and vitamin D supplements.

◀ Vegetarians who eat eggs, milk, cheese and other dairy products need to eat at least three servings a day.

A healthy vegetarian meal of pasta, vegetables and herbs. ▶

Get rid of the junk

Often, the foods that are easy to snack on are foods that can be bad for your health. Crisps, burgers and chips contain a lot of fat and salt. Sweets and fizzy drinks are packed with sugar. Read the list of ingredients on the can or packet. The nearer an ingredient is to the start of the list, the more of it there is in the food. Choose the snacks that have the least sugar, fat and salt.

▲ Eating burgers now and then is fine – it only becomes a problem if you eat them often.

Grabbing a snack

A lot of people like to grab a snack whenever they feel peckish. In some families, snacks have replaced regular meals such as breakfast, lunch and tea. There is nothing wrong with snacks, as long as you choose your snack carefully.

Choose the healthy option

There are healthy foods that you can choose for a quick snack. The list below gives you some ideas. Think about the way the food is cooked – grilled foods are healthier than fried foods.

FOOD	HEALTHIER CHOICE	ONLY EAT OCCASIONALLY
Fish	Grilled or baked	Fried and battered
Chicken	Skinless and grilled	Fried and coated in breadcrumbs or batter
Pizza	Vegetable toppings	Fatty toppings such as pepperoni, bacon and extra cheese
Vegetables and salads	Fresh, raw or steamed	Creamy dressings such as salad cream and mayonnaise
Potatoes	Baked	Chips, fried skins
Drinks	Juice, water, low-fat milk shakes, small sizes	Full-fat milk shakes, fizzy drinks, squashes, large sizes
Puddings	Fresh fruit, yoghurt, fruit salad	Doughnuts, cream cakes, fried apple pie

Healthy snacks can be part of a balanced diet.

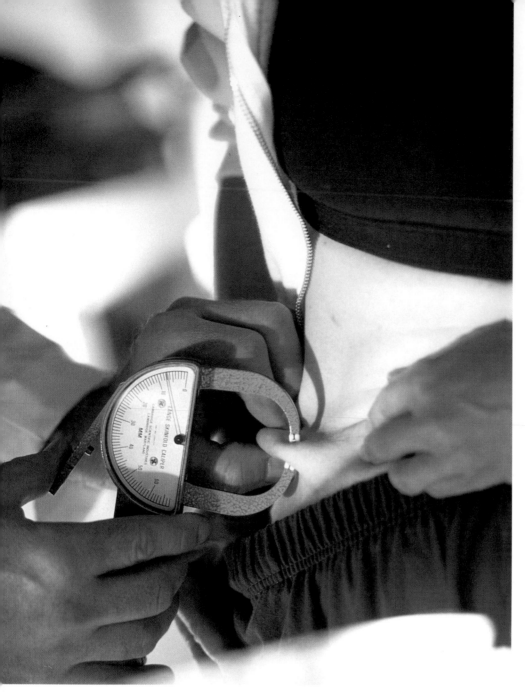

◀ In this picture the doctor is using callipers to pinch a patient's skin. This is a way of finding out how much body fat the patient has.

Weight problems

Being overweight puts extra strain on your body. It makes it harder for you to run around and enjoy sport and other activities. Your genes play a part in the way you put on weight. They affect the way your body stores fat and how fast you burn energy. People also tend to eat more when they are bored or miserable.

A healthy weight

Your doctor can tell you if you are the right weight for your age. If you are overweight, make sure you eat a well-balanced diet.

If you don't do much exercise, start off by doing 30 minutes of gentle exercise each day, such as walking or cycling. Try to do more vigorous exercise, such as running, swimming or dancing, at least twice a week.

You are likely to eat more and put on weight if you spend a lot of time in front of the TV or computer. ▼

DID YOU KNOW?

Adults who are overweight are more likely to get heart disease and diabetes than other people. Women who are very overweight have a higher risk of developing breast cancer.

41

Eating disorders

People who have anorexia nervosa eat very little food. They become very thin but they think they look fat. Anorexia is a very serious eating disorder. If people do not get the right treatment they may literally starve themselves to death.

People who have bulimia nervosa eat a huge amount of food in a short time. This is called a 'binge'. Then they make themselves sick, or take a laxative.

◀ People's natural body shapes vary. Some people look thin but are perfectly healthy.

▲ Counsellors try to help people understand the problems that have led to an eating disorder.

Stop or go? The traffic light test

RED – STOP!
Think before you eat these foods.
Are you eating too many of them?
Fatty foods: chips, crisps, butter, margarine, cream
Sugary foods: cakes, biscuits, sweets, chocolates, ice cream, sweet drinks

AMBER – SLOW DOWN
You need these foods for growth,
but go steady on them.
Protein foods: lean meat, fish, eggs, cheese, baked beans, nuts, dried peas and beans
Milk
Cereals: bread, cereals, pasta, rice

GREEN – GO!
Fill up on these nutritious foods.
Vegetables: raw, steamed, in salads
Fruit: fresh, frozen, canned in juice
Water

Treating disorders

Eating disorders sometimes develop because people are worried about the way they look. For other people, controlling the amount of food they eat is a way of dealing with deep unhappiness. People with eating disorders need help from specially trained counsellors and may need to spend time in hospital.

Food allergies

Some people are allergic to certain types of food. They might get a rash, wheezy breathing, a headache or a stomach upset. Their body reacts to the food as though it was an infection and starts fighting against it.

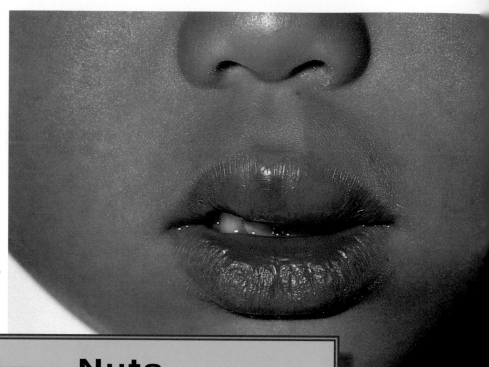

Nuts

Nuts can cause a serious allergic reaction in some people. Even a tiny amount of nut quickly makes them very ill. A condition called anaphylactic shock can develop and the person may die. They need an injection of adrenaline immediately. People who know they are at risk carry this medicine with them.

▲ This boy's lips have swollen up because he has had an allergic reaction to peanuts.

Dealing with allergies

Foods that sometimes cause allergies include milk and dairy products, wheat, eggs, shellfish, nuts and soya beans. The artificial colours and flavourings added to processed foods can cause allergic reactions as well.

If you think you have a food allergy, doctors can carry out tests to find out which foods are causing the problem. You might have to avoid that food for a while, then try it again in very small amounts.

◀ People who are allergic to peanuts sometimes eat them without knowing it. This is because peanut oil is often used to make cakes and biscuits.

Foods that often cause allergies

Food	Possible symptoms
Milk and dairy products, such as butter, ice cream, cheese and yoghurt	Diarrhoea, constipation, headache, eczema, pain in the abdomen
Gluten, which is found in flour, bread, biscuits, tinned and packet soups, stock cubes and processed foods	Headache and coeliac disease, which causes diarrhoea, weight loss and anaemia
Eggs, usually the white part used in meringues, mayonnaise and ice cream	Rashes, swelling, stomach upsets, asthma, eczema
Shellfish, such as prawns, shrimps, crabs and mussels	Stomach aches, headaches, feeling sick
Nuts, especially peanuts, walnuts and cashew nuts	Rashes, swelling, asthma, eczema. In severe cases, anaphylactic shock
Artificial colourings, flavourings and other chemicals in processed food	Wheezy breathing; possibly behaviour and learning problems.

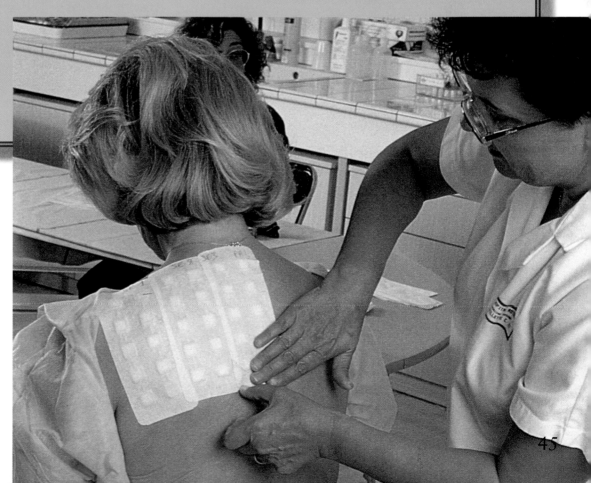

This woman is having a patch test to find out what is causing her allergy. Small amounts of different substances are put on her skin to find out if they cause an allergic reaction. ▶

Glossary

allergic reaction A collection of symptoms that show the body is trying to fight against a substance; for example, the runny eyes and sneezing of hay fever are an allergic reaction to pollen.

allergy Sensitivity to a substance that comes into contact with the body, through being eaten, drunk, or breathed in, or through touching the skin.

anaemia A disease in which the blood is not able to carry enough oxygen around the body to meet the body's needs; it makes people feel tired and weak.

asthma A disease that affects the lungs and makes it difficult for people to breathe.

calories The units used to measure the amount of energy in foods.

cell One of the body's 'building blocks'; there are many different kinds of cell – for example, cells making up organs such as the heart and brain, nerve cells, blood cells and bone cells.

cholesterol A waxy, fatty substance that is formed in the liver and found in egg yolks and animal fats.

clot (verb) To stick together; blood clots when you cut yourself, for example, so that you don't lose too much blood.

constipation Not being able to empty your bowels regularly.

eczema A skin problem that causes a sore, itchy rash.

game The meat from wild animals hunted for food, such as pheasant and venison (deer).

gelatine A substance produced by boiling animal skins and bones; it is used in jellies and many processed foods.

genes 'Instructions' that pass from the body of the parent to the child during reproduction. They control features such as eye colour, hair colour and height. They also influence whether a person develops certain diseases.

insoluble fibre Fibre that does not dissolve in the fluids inside your body, so it cannot be digested and absorbed.

laxative A medicine that makes you empty your bowels.

soluble fibre Fibre that can be partly broken down and absorbed by your body.

urine The waste liquid that passes out of your body when you go to the toilet.

Finding Out More

Books to read

Health Issues: Allergies by Sarah Lennard-Brown (Wayland, 2005)
Health Issues: Diabetes by Jo Whelan (Wayland, 2003)
Health Issues: Eating Disorders by Jo Whelan (Wayland, 2002)
Teen Issues: Diet by Joanna Kedge and Joanna Watson (Raintree, 2005)
Teen Issues: Fitness by Joanna Kedge and Joanna Watson (Raintree, 2005)

Useful Organizations

British Nutrition Foundation
High Holborn House
52-54 High Holborn
London WC1V 6RQ
Tel: 020 7404 6504
Fax: 020 7404 6747

The Dairy Council
Henrietta House, 17/18 Henrietta Street
London WC2E 8QH
Tel: 020 7395 4030
www.milk.co.uk/

Department of Health
www.lifebytes.gov.uk/indexmenu.html
The lifebytes interactive website is
designed specifically for young people
and covers a range of topics including
healthy eating, physical activity and
emotional well-being

Eating Disorders Association
103 Prince of Wales Road
Norwich NR1 1DW

Soil Association
Bristol House
40-56 Victoria Street
Bristol BS1 6BY
Tel: 0117 314 5000
Fax: 0117 314 5001

Index